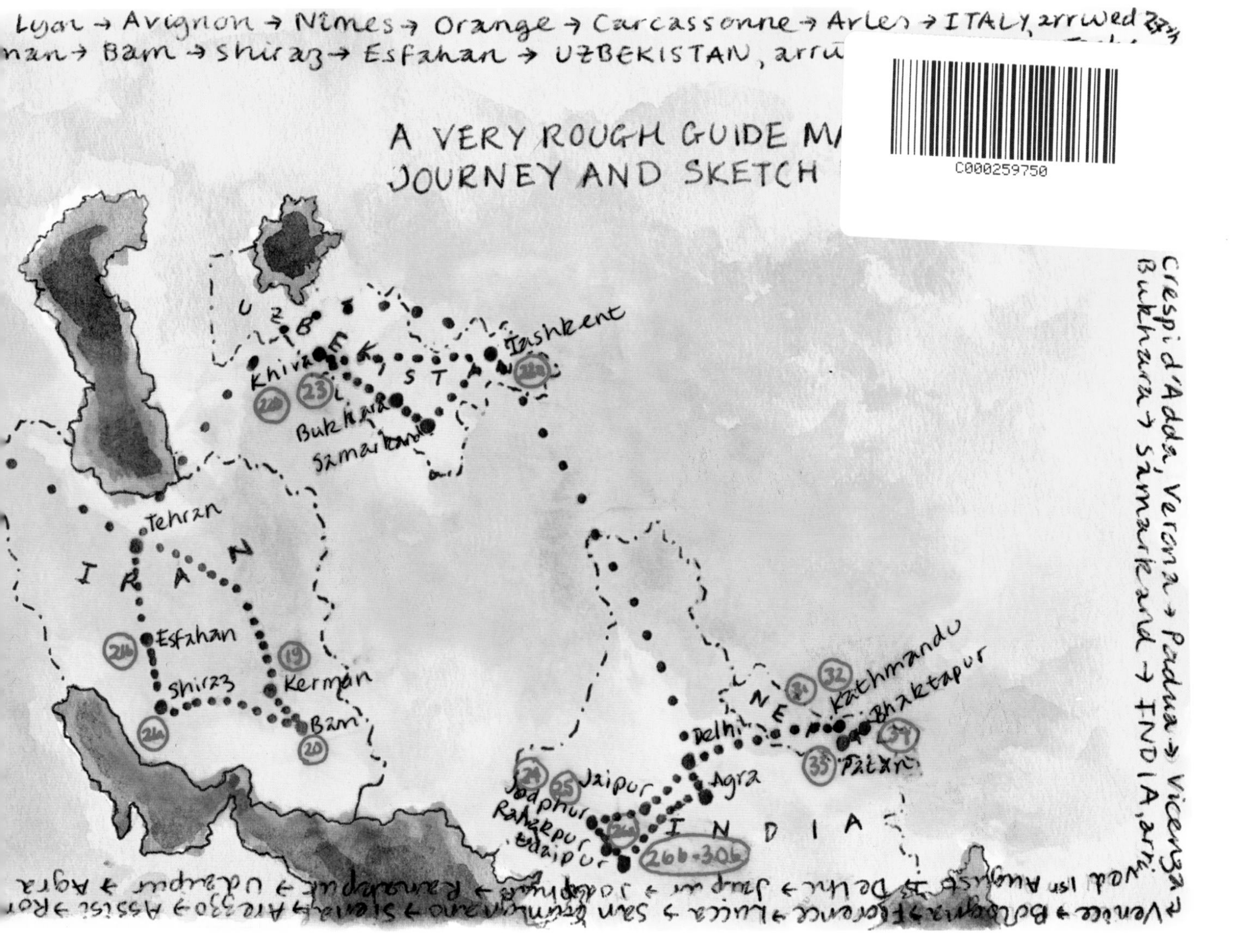

Lyon → Avignon → Nîmes → Orange → Carcassonne → Arles → ITALY, arrived
man → Bam → Shiraz → Esfahan → UZBEKISTAN, arri
A VERY ROUGH GUIDE MA
JOURNEY AND SKETCH
UZBEKISTAN
Tashkent
Khiva
Bukhara
Samarkand
Tehran
IRAN
Esfahan
Shiraz
Kerman
Bam
NE
Kathmandu
Bhaktapur
Patan
Delhi
Jaipur
Agra
Jodhpur
Ranakpur
Udaipur
INDIA
26b-30b
Crespi d'Adda, Verona → Padua → Vicenza
Bukhara → Samarkand → INDIA, arri

ACKNOWLEDGEMENTS

To my family and friends with love and much appreciation for all your help and support.

There are so many people to whom I would like to say a great big THANK YOU in the realisation of this book. I started to list everyone, found I was starting to write another book and beginning to sound like a Hollywood prize-winning acceptance speech. I was also worried about leaving someone's name out, which would be unforgiveable. So here is the heavily edited version:

Thank you to all my friends, whose help, contacts, references and advice were invaluable in the planning and preparation of my journey. Thank you also to all at the Winston Churchill Memorial Trust back in 2001 for enabling the journey and now in 2015 for your continued support.

Thank you to UNESCO UK (which sadly no longer exists), Women Welcome Women World Wide (5W) and the British Embassies for the moral support, contacts and 'on the ground' knowledge around the world which was invaluable. To all the friends, friends of friends and friends of friends of friends who provided shelter and warm hospitality on so much of my journey and special mention to Mum and Dad for being a fantastic 'mission control'.

Thank you to everyone who kept asking about the book and to my friends and other important people whose wisdom, patience and objectivity have ensured that the book has not turned out too badly.

And finally to you, most discerning and learned reader for picking out this book. THANK YOU!

Karen Neale, January 2015

The boring but important bits:

This edition first published in 2015

Text and Illustrations copyright © 2015 Karen Neale

Karen Neale has asserted her right under the Copyright, Designs and Patents Act, 1988 to be identified as the author, illustrator and designer of this work – it is my book – I did this!

ISBN: 978-0-9932111-0-2

A CIP catalogue for this book is available from the British Library

Scans of Sketches by Spiegl Press, Stamford, Lincolnshire

Printed in London, England (yes it is still possible to print books here) by the lovely printers: SPM, Rotherhithe, London SE16 3DH
www.spmprint.com

Still there? Now you can carry on and enjoy the book!

A FELLOW TRAVELLER

A Sketchbook Journey Inspired by
World Heritage Cities and Sites

Best wishes
Karen Neale

KAREN NEALE
Foreword by Nick Danziger

CONTENTS

Foreword

Introduction and a Few Words from WCMT

1   Paris, France

2   Haigerloch, Germany

3   Strasbourg, France

4   Avignon, France

5   Carcassonne, France

6   Milan, Italy

7   Venice, Italy

8   Lucca, Italy

9   Florence, Italy

10   San Gimignano, Italy

11   Siena, Italy

12   Assisi, Italy

13   Matera, Italy

14   Epidaurus, Greece

15a.   Hierapolis, Turkey

15b.   Ephesus, Turkey

16   Istanbul, (Grand Bazaar), Turkey

17   Istanbul, (Hagia Sophia and Blue Mosque) Turkey

18a.   Istanbul, (Inside the Hagia Sophia), Turkey

18b.   Istanbul, (The Spice Market),Turkey

19a.   Kerman, (James Mosque), Iran

19b.   Kerman, (Bazaar), Iran

20   Arg-e-Bam, Iran

21a.   Shiraz, Iran

21b.   Esfahan, Iran

22a.   Tashkent, Uzbekistan

22b.   Khiva, Uzbekistan

23   Khiva, Uzbekistan

24   Jodphur, (Surajpol, Meherengarh Fort), India

25   Jodphur, (Ramparts of Meherengarh Fort), India

26a.   Ranakpur, India

26b.   Udaipur, (The Tailor) India

27   Udaipur, (View across Lake Pichola), India

28   Udaipur, (Krishna's Birthday), India

29   Udaipur, (View from Jagmandir Island), India

30a.   Udaipur, (View from the Paper Shop), India

30b.   Udaipur, (Women Washing), India

31   Kathmandu, (Durbar Square), Nepal

32a.   Kathmandu, (from the Royal Palace), Nepal

32b.   Kathmandu, (Swayambunath Temple), Nepal

33   Kathmandu, (Unfinished), Nepal

34   Bhaktapur, Nepal

Edited Extracts of the Words around the Sketches

And a Final Word...

FOREWORD

I first met Karen when she was shortlisted for a Winston Churchill Memorial Trust Fellowship. Until then I had been more used to sitting on Karen's side of the table, being interviewed rather than being the person asking the questions. In my position now on the interview panel as an advisory council member, I was the poacher turned gamekeeper.

Karen's interview took place well over a decade ago, but in the intervening years there are some interviewees you never forget and Karen has been one of them. I was struck by her passion and her courage. Her passion was evident in the way she spoke about her project and her work. Her courage was in the proposed ambitious plan of going to parts of the world that in many instances had disappeared from most tourists' itineraries.

I am sure that as you leaf through this album of watercolours inspired by World Heritage Cities and Sites you will immediately be drawn in by the soul and personal vision of an artist who can communicate something of both place and time. You may also find – as did I – that your favourites stir memories of your own visit to that particular location.

For me, Karen has captured the essence of both nearby places such as Venice and remote cities like Bam in Iran, which has the additional layer of poignancy because of the earthquake which destroyed much of what you see in her portrait of the Citadel, its buildings and ramparts*. As for those locations I haven't visited, her personal annotations help me to fill in the gaps and the spirit of those places.

I hope this album will be enjoyed both for the pleasure of visiting these places and also for the language that Karen has created with pen and brush.

Nick Danziger
On location, Northern Uganda, December 2014
www.nickdanziger.com

Although badly damaged in the 2003 earthquake, substantial areas of the Citadel have survived and are being sympathetically restored.

INTRODUCTION

My passion is sketching and painting the world around me. A Fellow Traveller is a sketchbook diary of my journey inspired by UNESCO* World Heritage Cities and Sites as a Churchill Fellow. I was awarded my WCMT** Travelling Fellowship in 2001, leaving London in April that year and travelling for five months through France, Italy, Greece, Turkey, Iran, Uzbekistan, India and Nepal. During this time I completed 106 annotated, watercolour sketches recording my experience, 42 of which appear in this book.

It was in 2000, while working as an architect in London, when I came across the UNESCO World Heritage List, that the idea for my journey began to crystallize. This list designates sites as having properties of outstanding universal value, and if you haven't seen it, take a look, as it is an amazing record of our global cultural and natural heritage.

Inspired by the list, I soon began to plan my adventure with a few self-imposed parameters to make the journey viable. These included my limited budget, the length of time I wanted to be away from home, and the fact that I would always try to travel as much as possible in a continual direction on 'terra firma' and a little 'aqua' so as to see the cultural connections gradually unfold. Being awarded a Churchill Travelling Fellowship not only took away any financial worries, it also opened doors and gave my journey more purpose.

This truly was a journey of a lifetime. My sketchbook, which was my 'fellow traveller' was also my passport to people and places. When standing or if lucky, sitting somewhere for several hours, simply drawing with just a black BIC biro, I became a part of that place for a time. Sketching erodes cultural and linguistic barriers, as a picture and the process to create it can be universally understood. Almost without exception, people were friendly, informative, inquisitive and afforded me great hospitality. I soon realised that despite our different cultures, languages, societal and physical structures, there lies a common universal aspiration. That is to lead an uncomplicated, peaceful life, with a roof over one's head, food on the table and to be surrounded by family and friends, and taking great pride in our natural and cultural heritage.

Inside the front cover of this book lies the map of my journey. The pages that follow contain a selection of my sketches, some designated sites, some not. The final section combines the pictures with edited extracts of the words around them.

The world is continually changing and I was very fortunate to travel when I did. The sketches are not only about capturing the buildings, monuments and landscapes, but also recording at that point in time, their context, the people and the bustle of every day life in these places – humanity in its heritage. I hope that you will enjoy the adventure.

Karen Neale, January 2015

*   *United Nations Educational, Scientific and Cultural Organization*
     www.whc.unesco.org
***Winston Churchill Memorial Trust (see next page)*

A FEW WORDS FROM THE WINSTON CHURCHILL MEMORIAL TRUST

As the national memorial and living legacy of Sir Winston Churchill, we fund British citizens to travel the world in search of new ideas and innovative solutions to the challenges facing today's society. On return they are charged with sharing these ideas as widely as possible, to contribute to the improvement of this country at a local, regional and national level.

The award of a Churchill Fellowship, as it is known, can have a profound impact. Fellows return with a greater belief in their own abilities, and with a reignited passion for their work. Often a Fellowship serves as a catalyst that unlocks potential and accelerates careers, and continues to be a motivating influence long after the travels are over. The emphasis of a Fellowship is not only on the development of the individual, but also on the wider benefits that they can achieve through the ideas with which they return.

Karen's interview panel was an illustrious one consisting as it did of Nick Danziger (a Churchill Fellow himself and author of the foreword of this book), Sir Terence English (who performed the first successful heart transplant in the UK) and Sir Roger Bannister (who ran the first sub-four minute mile in 1952 as a junior doctor, and went on to become a neurologist of renown). Her Fellowship was an unusual one for us, but presented with a project that promised to share our incredible global heritage through travel and painting, two things of such importance to Churchill himself, we could hardly turn her down, and nor did we want to.

We are delighted that our panel had the foresight to make Karen a Churchill Fellow. It has been very rewarding for us to watch her career evolve from architect to artist, triggered by this journey, and see her find success in her new field.

We are truly thrilled that she has chosen to publish her Fellowship sketchbook (her fourth publication), in our 50th Anniversary year. It is particularly fitting as when painting in both Avignon and Carcassonne she was following in Churchill's footsteps, since he had painted similar views in both places, just a few decades earlier.

This is a perfect gem of a book and we hope you enjoy Karen's journey as much as we have, through her wonderful sketches, encircled and brought alive by her marvellous diary entries.

For information on how to apply for a Churchill Fellowship visit **www.wcmt.org.uk**

1

Wednesday 11th April 2007 - back again in Haigerloch, Germany to see Jane and family. Still as picturesque - really stunning

was a long but very beautiful journey driving through the Black Forest - really

and keeps well. I am dying to start raining, so that explains why there is so much rain! It

talking to on the train said to me (and sorry for uncovered German spelling)

Wenn die Engeln verreisen, weil der Himmer trauer, in ihre Weiso when the Engels travel, the Anglos travel, the

Thursday 12th April 2001. Well here I am in Strasbourg, coming back on a different but equally beau
the main island...—

with their steeply sloping roofs, supposedly used for drying hides and also

marking the start of Petite France — the little island which used to be the former tanners', dyeing and

through the dark silent and misty pines of the Schwarzwald. And on my eighth day it is finally not

raining. Still very cold though and I was sitting on top of the pons couvert —

covered bridge, looking back at the four massive 13th century square towers (used to be part of the city's

3

Tuesday 17th April 2001 – Avignon ~ hurrah the sky is blue, the sun is shining but ooch, there is a rain tourist count today!

kingdom of France and the Holy Roman Empire, it still commands a healthy

The river Rhône is very high as indeed have been all the rivers I have s

I have instated a healthy respect for this Papal town and famous crossing between the then p

racing down the Rhône Valley and there's nowhere to hide. Fearlessly into the wind I head across the exposed Pont de Bénézet Daladier to the Île de la Barthe

← two weeks in France – very very high indeed, but Pont d'Avignon is still standing as is the Palais des Papes —

← to enjoy this masterly view, as can imagine that seven hundred years ago this imposing ↑

Sunday 22nd April 2001 - standing on the pont Neuf looking across to le Pont Vieux and...

thoughts of the more friendly and preferable onslaught of tourists...

Carcassonne is a wonderful place ~ or two really the tourist trading contained in the walled city and the everyday trading

...ackground the cité, the amazingly preserved walled city. This is largely due to Viollet le Duc, and

2 Carcassonne scholar Jean-Pierre Cros-Mayrevieille who both

5

opposed successfully the decree of 1850 to demolish all of the fortifications. I'm sure Viollet de

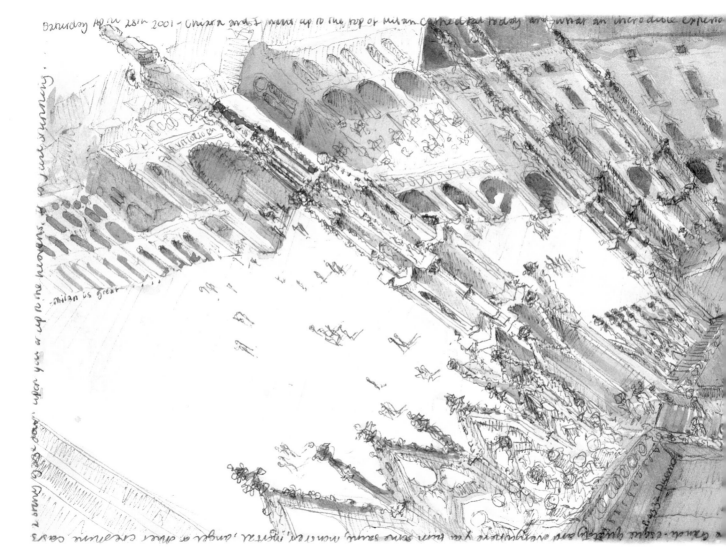

Saturday April 28th 2001 - Chiara and I went up to the top of Milan Cathedral today and what an incredible experience.

Milan is great.

after you a up in the heavens, it is interesting.

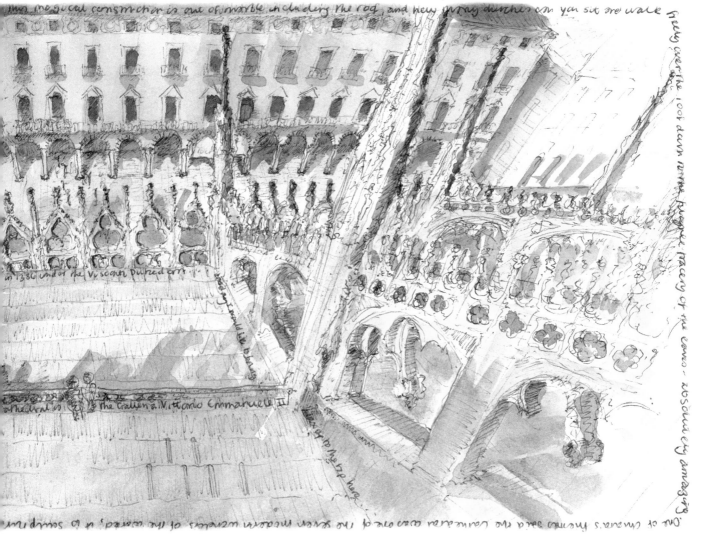

this medieval construction is one of marble including the roof, and how many churches can you sit and walk

freely over the 100 ft down to the people. Tracery of the cows – absolutely amazing

in 1386 end of the Visconti Dukedom

this is I would like to be up

the vault of the Galleria Vittorio Emmanuele II

they'll be here

Friday 4th May 2001 — a little trip on the train for just a few hours in magical Venice. I could
thousands every day and even more pigeons!

more happily St Marks Square in sunshine gorgeous as ever represented by thousands

more amazed, but which would have given the difference I piazza almost between like and dark as so very age

...ting lost down all the alleys, arriving at a canal, going back down alleys, eventually find a bridge across the canal, and so on. I walked through the Jewish ghetto which was perso...

7

Wednesday 9th May 2001 - Arrived in Florence yesterday from Bologna, I have been so well looked after in Italy a

And the famous piazza Anfiteatro lived up to all my expectations - it

looks, there is just so much here to draw. We be delighted in... with running these place I will come back to!

Thursday May 10th 2001, walked up to the top of the hotel Macchiavelli where mum and dad are staying nearby which we have been thoroughly enjoying . . . .

the amazing view of San Lorenzo, which is around the corner from the hotel, with its old and new sacristy by Brunelleschi and Michelangelo, the Duomo beyond, Castle Vecchio and a whole

host of other baroque buildings, which make up Florence's famous skyline. I don't think this particular view

9

Sunday 13th May 2001; Dan drove me across the beautiful Tuscan hills from home where you could see

it is easy to understand why so many people love this place and the world such as Dan's parents who live overlooking the beautiful isolated house overlooking the fields which could b seen for miles...

the Cathedral and into Piazza Duomo...

as you walk through this square into the other

tourist-drenched in Tuscany, which I can well believe - and probably quite justifiably

of San Gimignano

Monday 14th May 2001; Dan the man dropped me off in dear old Siena. Climbed up the steep hill, throug

alleys which always take the picturesque route rather than a direct one and then there you are

in the Piazza del Campo, and this time it didn't rain. I have been in two

different trips before and the rain came along too. This time the clouds threatened but this time the

Friday 18th May 2001 - well I have really outdone myself this time walking up and down steep hills and within it.

Friday 18th May 2001 - well I have really outdone myself this time walking up and down steep hills and within it. [text along left margin, rotated] stay down to Basilica San Francisco which has a celestial beauty about

alleys to find this sketch and my legs are letting me know about it! Well this view is from Rocca

Minore, looking across to Rocca Maggiore · Rocca Minore really is quite

frescoes by the ...

incredible frescoes

12

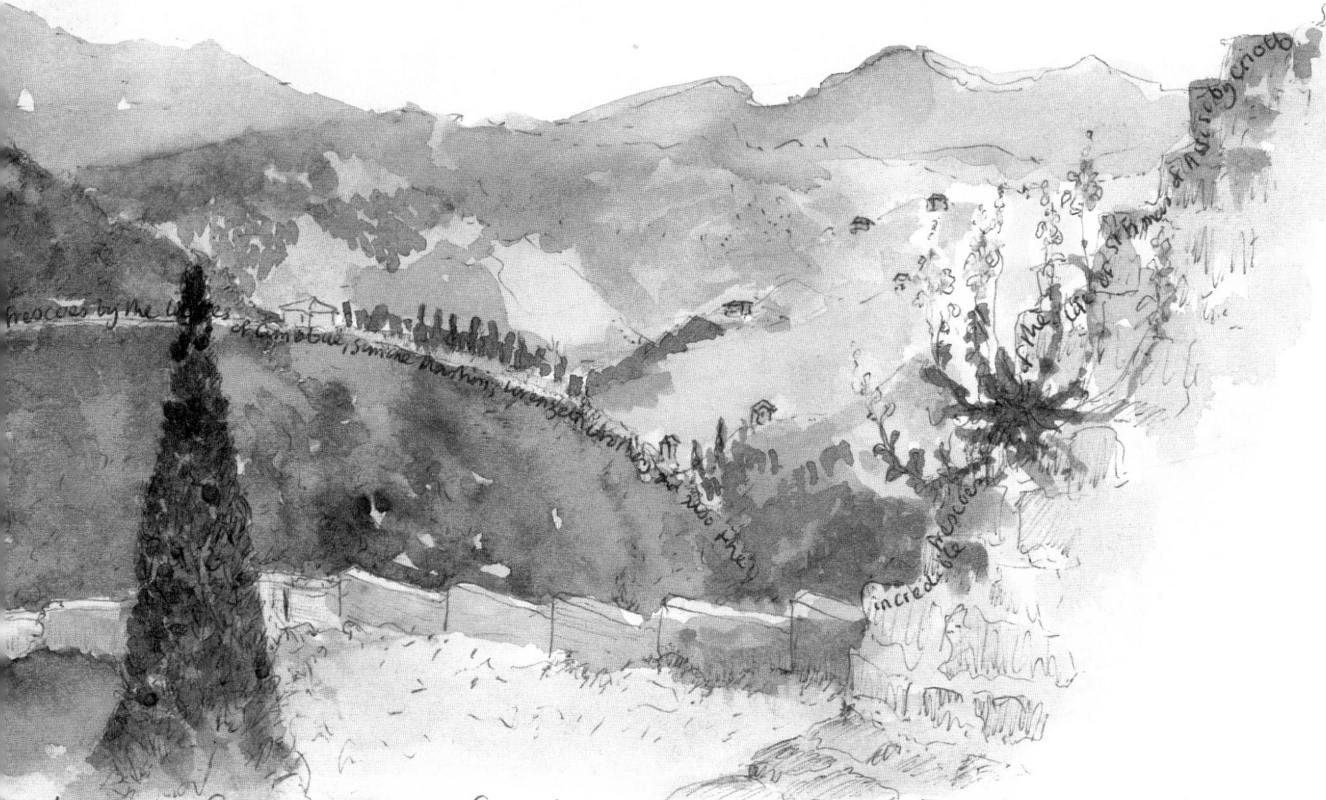

Sunday 27th May 2001 ~ Matera, a truly incredible place, and the dogs of this area are extremely fr

The mad swallows swooping overhead in eternal circles like an airy whirlpool of mirthfull mayhem. wonderful

In a couple of days I leave this country. I shall miss Italy. I feel very at home here and I've received such wonderfully warm hospitality from friends, friends of friends, and friends of friends of friends. They've been so good to me and of course made Italy even more rewarding

and Matera is so completely spellbinding maybe because it is understated, not hyped up, not yet on the major tourist pilgrimage routes, but I wonder in ten years time, ... But I think it can carry it very well.

...ss his home: In Matera dogs appear snoozing at the top of a building overlooking the like a gargoyle and welcome you to Matera in comical fashion: 2kes is the

lish women, yesterday in Ferrandini station, whilst waiting for the bus to take me to Matera, the

station dog did, limping, cuddly and snuggly, come over; rolled over and demanded

across in Sassi Caveoso and at daime p.m. there is San Pietro Cave ... and Madonna deli Idris sets into the rocks... all quite amazing.

un running as I rubbed the stationmaster said the station was open and offered a space but I thought I

13

Saturday 2nd June 2001 - on the bus from Nafplio to Epidaurus . . . . .

Now I wasn't sure what to expect of Epidavros, yet another ancient theatre, but Epidavros is really something truly spectacular. The acoustics are indeed near perfect. You can indeed here a penny drop on the centre circle of the stage and hear it on the back row, when someone who does know how to sing, sings it is beautiful. And the setting could really not be more spectacular. When Polykleitos built this in the fourth century B.C. I wonder if he realized my idea that two and a half thousand years later people from around the world would still be coming here to be amazed at this absolute wonder. People from Taiwan and Puerto Rico are sat here with me waiting for the local bus to take us back to Nafplio. They are all amazed and it is this incredible place. It is part of the ancient Sanctuary dedicated to The healing god Asclepius. The theatre can hold 14,000 people and is so much a part of its natural surroundings, it was only rediscovered in the nineteenth century). Apparently because of so much care with all the mathematical precision that it even blends seamlessly into its hillside setting. How did he did new surroundings be achieved. To me it really is a wonder of the world. So much incredible... to learn from them

Sunday 17th June 2001 — well up beyond the terraces and the ruins of Hierapolis — about three or four hundred metres

demonstrating the warmth of...

This is Kezban Acat — a very lively lady

...ly up in the mountains during summer. This is...

...gets me at last. They make carpets over the ...... from the sheeps wool...... there is a very ......

Truly wonderful

15a

Tuesday 19th June 2001 ~ Arrived in Selçuk yesterday and today in between the rain clouds (how can this be) I am drawing in Ephesus the city.

I am drawing in Efeo in Ephesus - which is quite amazing. The library is and have

been an obvious choice - an amazing view there - and the temple of Hadrian was equally impressive with Arian

15b

Saturday June 23rd 2001 — finally in Istanbul — and lost in the wonderful and bustling Grand bazaar — an experience —

You can buy just about everything here I think — for a price and the antique pewter, copper, gold don't come cheap

It's great here — I may drink the bazaar's Turkish tea remembering though, as I can't speak one *word* of Turkish.

issed - this has got to be one of the most amazing places that I have seen so far, and it is sketcher's paradise overload.

It has taken me four hours to draw this let alone paint it, and the vas majority of people here

TERZILER SOKAK

are extraordinary friendly, and keep me plied with water and lemon tea - which is very hospitable. It's a real place

16

Thursday 28th June 2001 — so into my new sketchbook and a little over half way through my journey.

one of the fabulous views all around Istanbul, this one being from the top of the lovely hotel Poem looking at the Blue Mosque and the Hagia Sophia standing at each other

across the Istanbul rooftops. Istanbul is comparatively inexpensive - wonderful people - come + draw!

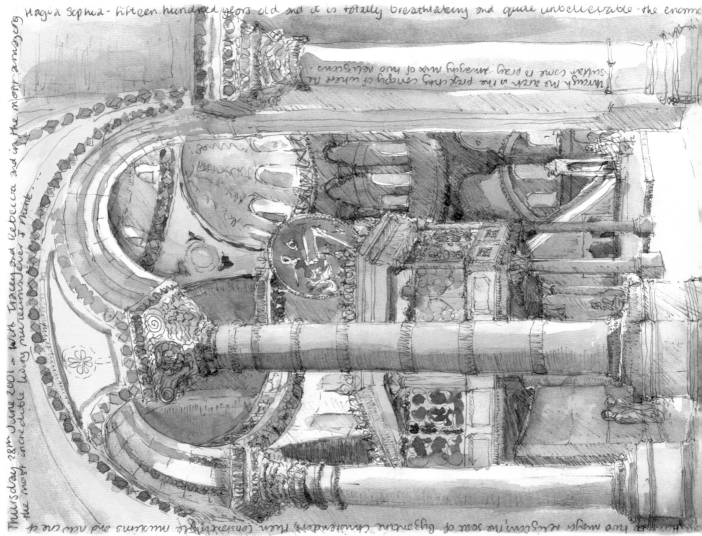

Hagia Sophia - fifteen hundred years old and it is totally breathtaking and quite unbelievable - the enorm

Thursday 28th June 2001 - with Tracey and Rebecca and in the most amazing the most incredible living museum ever I think.

18a

APHRODISIAQUE
DES
SULTANS
MESIR MACUNU

BAHARATÇI
41//

SOFT
YOSUN
A-BUNU

KINA

KINA
HENNA

18b

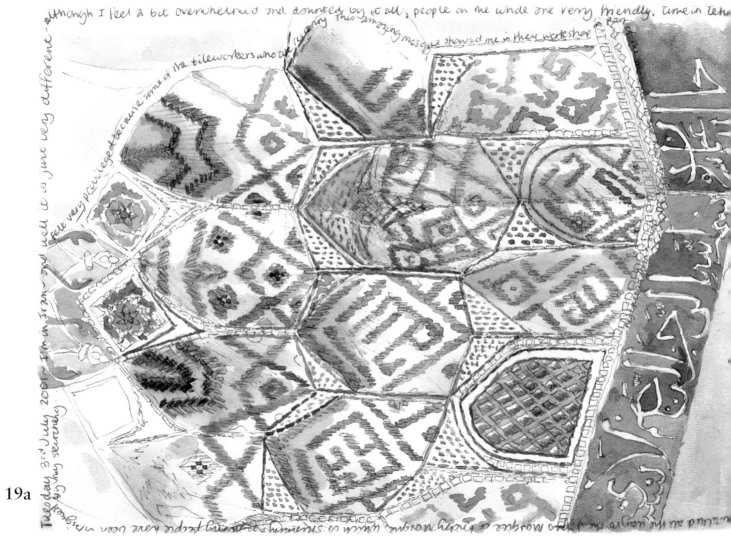

although I feel a bit overwhelmed and daunted by it all, people on the whole are very friendly. Time in Teh...

of the tileworkers who are restoring this amazing mosque showed me in their workshop

felt very privileged because some

Tuesday 3rd July 2001 - I'm in Iran and well it is just very different -

by any secretary

19a

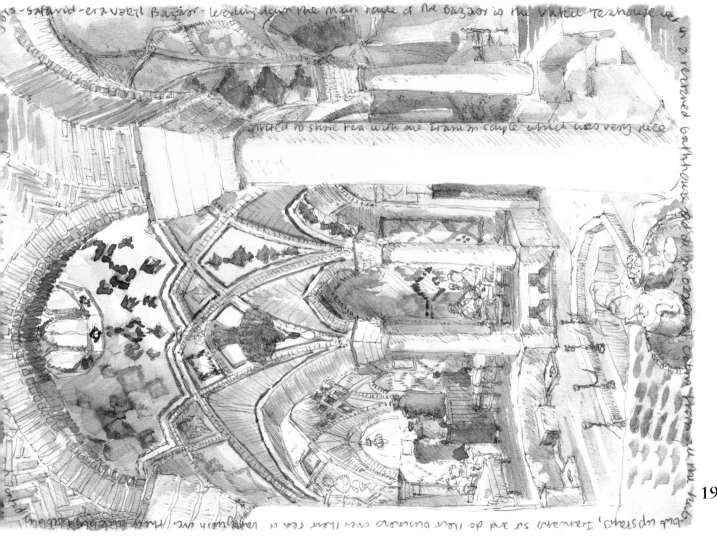

...s-Safavid-era Vakil Bazaar. Leading down the main route of the bazaar is the Vakil Teahouse, set in a restored bathhouse...

tried to share tea with an Iranian couple which was very nice

19b

Thursday 5th July 2001 - arrived yesterday across the desert to apparently three million palm trees forming th

compelling, even while drawing this at 50° early in the morning, making

the poor and sick lived over here

This is the bazaar. No a

d the town of Bam. The modern day city new lives outsides the walls of the ancient city Arg-e Bam. the

the whole adventure to Bam has been quite magical staying at Mr Akbar's weird

this was the middle class moving to suburbia

teahouse

y inhabitants new in this amazing ancient city are
the restoration works, their ladies at the teahouse in the gatehouse to the citadel (great cooked eggs!)
e odd ... curious ... lizard and bird.

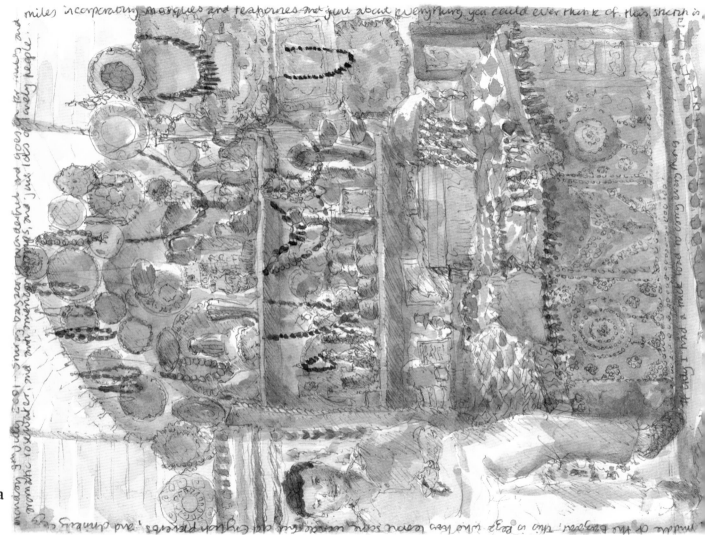

miles incorporating mosques and teahouses and just about everything you could ever think of. this sketch is

21a

...haps the most stunning place I've visited in Iran, and Tabriz Square is a town planning jewel nonetheless. I think it is about 500m by 160m, not completely arcaded with a plethora of shop...

The arcade? Suddenly the symphony of clanging metal gets louder and louder and then you turn the corner and it is the coppersmiths' bazaar and their amazing men, many of them white clad are busily crafting their amazing pots and in this din you can see all the pings of small bowls brilliant.

21b

Sunday 15th July 2001 — 2u change and to Tashkent, Uzbekistan, and all of a

22a

22b

23

I know it is just a whole different way of being, thinking and doing — and keep trying to tell myself that

24

Thursday 9th August 2001 ~ High up on the ramparts of the Meher

...rs, I think I was close to the 1 chapel gate (in) famous for the fifteen handprints next to it dedicating the sati marks of the Maharaja Man Singh's widows who threw themselves on his funeral pyre in 1843 - gruesome. It seems to me 150 years that remains very

26A

Friday 10th August 2001 — so in decadent style I left Jodhpur today for

Bumpy incredible — ?

Remember to draw the Jain temples in India. Superb free by a form of marble

26B

Monday 13th August to Friday 17th August (mum and dad's anniversary) Well this is the amazing

a beautiful view as this with some of the *Madhur* and things just around the corner.

gory but have met some lovely people who have made it easier. I find it difficult in meeting such

the top of the Kankarwa Haveli where I am staying, and I've been drawing this in between rain showers and hot sunshine. This Haveli has been my sanctuary and

refuge the city which has made me use away back home. I still find

Udaipur the city which has made me use away back home. I still find

27

it is Khrishna's birthday today, although I got wildly different answers as to how old he was~ but suffice

Monday 13th August 2001 - what an incredible day today here in Udaipur, I am absolutely feverished completely mad I am amazed there were no serious ... the best views. ~ pyramids collapsed one after another, until the bottom be circle ~ not for the claustrophobic ~ lucky p.g. in our lives so each ... anything the circle ~ not for the bottom was lowered a little and then one daring team grabbed the pot.

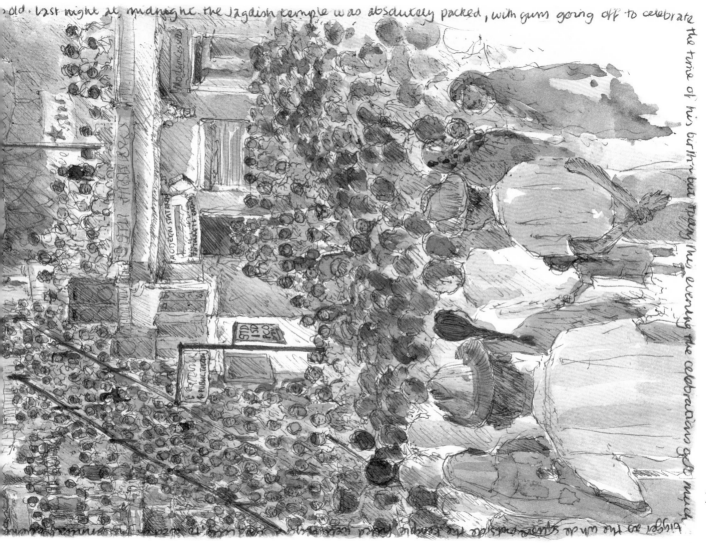

...old. Last night at midnight the Jagdish temple was absolutely packed, with guns going off to celebrate the time of his birth but they (his evening the celebration got much bigger as the whole town...

28

looking for the missing English girl - even though I had told the boat man that I would return later. Anyway all

was fine, just sat on a jetty near the city palace and enjoyed watching the whole...

Wednesday August 15th 2001 - a very atmospheric monsoon day today. Took a boat ride out on the serene lan...

...ola to Jagmandir island just in time as the heavens opened and the dark clouds leapt over the mountains announced and shrouding the landscape in mysterious mist. It had been a few hours of rare calmness here in me. only Europeans from a few other palace Indians and a waiter and a guard

have a little refuge from which I can capture the chaos out in the street; people, animals, vehicles

30a

way because I feel I have just started to get a little more of a taste of life in India beyond the

hassle. It is still an assault on all the senses, all of the time. But from

the safe haven of the lovely Ramasami hotel you can look down to the Ghat, the women washing

Campion throw themselves in swimming

30b

Friday, Saturday August 24th/25th 2001 + country number nine, and although I am quite worn out now, I think.

monkeys and mosquitoes making mischief. A monkey climbed one of the roofs and pushed down tiles smashing on the ground, whilst the mosquitoes simply concentrated on me!

worth the wait and all the effort! Although with as much perseverance and more preposterously this...

the Royal Palace

sacred cows being sacred!

much gentler, calmer pace here and every...

Friday August 24th 2001 The view from the eighth of the nine storied Basantapur tower of the Royal Palace looking across Nasal chowk to Panch Mukhi Hanuman temple

32a

nday 26th August 2001 - a walk out of the city and up three hundred and sixty five gravity defying stone steps to a few minutes, and amazingly we just looked at each other. I said he couldn't have my book and he just

I thought by coming to a temple it would be a little more peaceful... but far from it! The angelic looking cheeky kids, and then the real monkeys (great game with the kids "you're the monkey!... no you're the monkey...") grown ups, pigeons - one with a token gesture landing on my signed sketchbook, all the jolly looking tibetan prints in their various shades of red wine coloured oleo oh and the ... odd tourist -- so no wonder this was very

swung in beneath a more appropriately the monkey temple the monkeys looked me up and down and sat there...

difficult to
draw, still I very
much enjoyed the
entertaining trek up
here - a long old street
after a short street

hills (well a short terms.)

32b

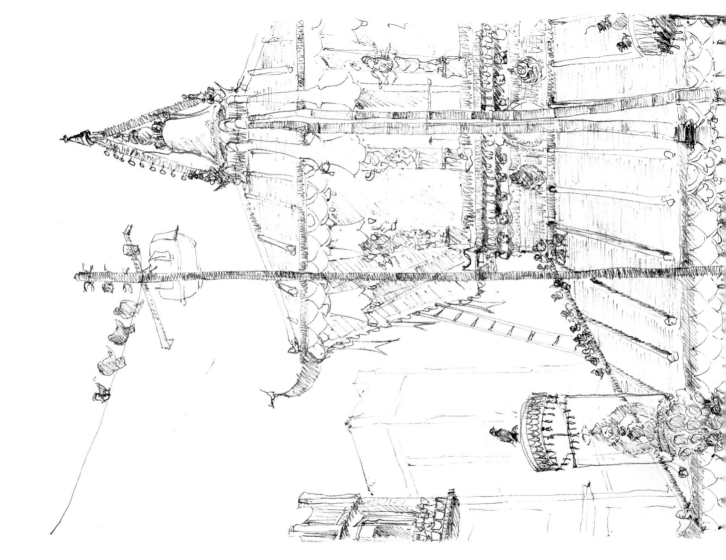

33

Amazing Italian tourists quibbling over a quid in the little guesthouse here (and they are really in the wrong) while I discover that the little boy who works here does not really have parents and he is earning money to try and get himself back to school. It all just does not add up.

and si nestled in the foothills which seem much closer than Kathmandu. This is

Taumadi Tole, probably the oldest part of town today, from the paved plaza of Taumadi Tole on

EDITED EXTRACTS OF THE WORDS AROUND THE SKETCHES

The map of my journey shows all the places I visited and the numbers indicate the 42 sketches shown in this book. As previously mentioned the World Heritage List was the inspiration for my journey. Along the way I saw countless precious places that are not on the list, but had to be drawn.

Some of them are in this book as an indelible and interwoven part of the journey. Everywhere in the world we are never far from magical places and the World Heritage List highlights the most prominent ones and keeps us aware how precious and fragile our world is...

1. Paris, France Saturday 7th April 2001

So here it is, the Panthéon, the first sketch of my 'grand voyage.' I don't think it has quite sunk in that the journey which I have been planning for so long is actually happening. It is as cold in Paris as it was in London and has rained most of the time. This has made it a challenge for me to sketch all the outside spaces that I wanted to, such as Mr. Pei's crystalline pyramid at the Louvre or the Musée d'Orsay covered in shrouds and scaffolding. Still an early start today ensured I got here before the heavens opened. It is also very quiet here compared with much of central Paris.

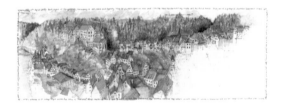

2. Haigerloch, Germany Wednesday 11th April 2001

Popped over the border into Germany and to Haigerloch, where I'm staying with friends on my way to Strasbourg. It is still as picturesque as ever, and still the rain has followed my route into the Black Forest! A German teacher whom I got talking to on the train said to me: 'Wenn die Engel vereisen, weint der Himmel tränen'. In other words: 'When the angels travel, the Heavens shed tears.' Well, I am doing a rather large journey, so that explains why there is so much rain.

3. Strasbourg, France Thursday 12th April 2001

Well here I am in Strasbourg and on the eighth day of my trip it is finally not raining. It is still very cold though, as I sit here on the top of Les Ponts Couverts – the covered bridges – looking back to the massive 13th Century square towers that used to be part of this city's defences. The towers mark the start of La Petite France – the little island which is the former tanners' district. The steeply sloping roofs of the houses were supposedly used for drying the tanned hides...

4. Avignon, France Sunday 17th April 2001

Avignon – hurrah the sky is blue and the sun is shining, but boo there is a raw north wind racing down the Rhône Valley and there's nowhere for me to hide. Fearlessly into the wind I head across the exposed Pont Édouard Daladier to the Île de la Barthelasse, to enjoy this incredible view. This imposing site must have instilled a healthy respect for this papal town and frontier crossing between the then kingdom of France and the Holy Roman Empire. It still commands a healthy tourist count today.

5. Carcassonne, France Sunday 22nd April 2001

Standing on le Pont Neuf looking across to le Pont Vieux and the imposing background of the Cité, the amazingly preserved walled city. The fact I can draw this view is largely due to the efforts of the conservation architect Viollet-le-Duc and a Carcassonne Scholar Jean-Pierre Cros-Mayrevieille who both successfully opposed a decree by the French state in 1850 to demolish this fortified town. I hope the tourist industry in Carcassonne appreciate their prophetic efforts.

6. Milan, Italy Saturday 28th April 2001

I climbed to the top of Milan Cathedral today and what an incredible experience it was. The whole of this magical construction is out of marble. How many churches can you sit on the roof of or walk freely down to the filigree tracery of the eaves? Absolutely amazing! It is sculptural in a pre-Gaudíesque way and everywhere you turn some saint, monster, mortal, angel or other creature casts a stony gaze down upon you or up to the heaven. It is just stunning.

7. Venice, Italy Friday 4th May 2001

I could spend years getting lost in Venice's alleyways, arriving at a canal, going back up another alley until eventually finding a bridge over the canal and so on. I walked through the Jewish Ghetto, which was powerfully moving, crossing the bridge only a few metres away. It is humbling to think the same bridge probably meant the difference between life and death not so long ago… More happily, St. Mark's Square is still as gorgeous as ever. Appreciated by thousands of people every day – and even more pigeons.

8. Lucca, Italy Wednesday 9th May 2001

I arrived in Florence yesterday from Bologna. I have been so well looked after in Italy, staying with such lovely people every day since I arrived. I visited Ferrara on Monday, which I just could not sketch, despite its beauty. Anyway today I feel I could stay in Lucca for weeks, there is so much here to draw and be delighted in. It is simply another place I will have to come back to! Lucca's famous Piazza dell'Anfiteatro lived up to all my expectations...

9. Florence, Italy Thursday May 10th 2001

I walked up to the top of this Florentine hotel and found an amazing view of San Lorenzo, with its old and new sacristy by Brunelleschi and Michelangelo, Il Duomo beyond, Palazzo Vecchio and a whole host of other fabulous buildings, which make up Florence's famous skyline.
I don't think this view has featured on too many postcards. This is an amazing part of Florence, just around the corner from the massive main market hall and many excellent eating establishments...

10. San Gimignano, Italy Sunday 13th May 2001

As we drove towards San Gimignano, I caught site of its medieval skyscraper-outline across the beautiful Tuscan Hills. I find it quite unique and beautiful, without stepping into tweedom. This is sketched from the Torre Grossa, the largest and tallest of the fourteen remaining towers. There were originally seventy two in the Middle Ages, when San Gimignano was a prosperous little trading town. Just over half of the towers have made it into this piccie.

11. Siena, Italy Monday 14th May 2001

Having climbed up a steep hill through the winding alleys, which always take a picturesque route rather than a direct one, I found myself here in the Piazza del Campo. I have been on two daytrips to Siena before and the rain has always come along too. But this time, although the clouds threatened, they showed mercy. After drawing this I sat in one of the bars on the piazza for an aperitivo with a friend who works here and thought about how wonderful a place it was to be in...

12. Assisi, Italy Friday 18th May 2001

I have outdone myself this time, walking up and down steep hills to find this sketch and my legs are letting me know about it. This view is from Rocca Minore, looking across to Rocca Maggiore. Unfortunately you can't see the Basilico di San Francesco, which has a celestial beauty about and within it. The Basilico is adorned with gorgeous paintings by the likes of Cimabue, Simone Martini, the Lorenzetti brothers and is also home to Giotto's frescoes of the life of St Francis of Assisi.

13. Matera, Italy Sunday 27th May 2001

Matera is a truly incredible place carved out of the soft tufo rocks. In Matera dogs appear suddenly at the top of buildings, like furry gargoyles to welcome you in comical fashion. This is the view from Palazzo Lanfranchi, looking across to Sasso Caveoso, with il Duomo on the left. Also here are San Pietro Caveoso and Madonna dell'Idris set into the rocks. The mad swallows swooping overhead in eternal circles like an airy whirlpool of mirthful mayhem add to the wonder of the scene.

14. Epidaurus, Greece Saturday 2nd June 2001

In a small valley in the Peloponnesus, the ancient theatre of Epidaurus is to me, truly a wonder of the world. Polykleitus built this in the 4th Century BC and the acoustics are near perfect – from the back tier you can hear a penny, or rather a drachma, drop on the centre circle of the stage. The site is part of an ancient sanctuary dedicated to the healing god Asklepios and blends into its natural surrounding so well it was only rediscovered in the 19th century.

15a. Hierapolis, Turkey Sunday 17th June 2001
Up beyond the extraordinary natural terraces and ruins of Hierapolis is a semi-nomadic village in which they make carpets during the winter from local sheep's wool, as demonstrated here.

15b. Ephesus, Turkey Tuesday 19th June 2001
Here in Ephesus or Efes at the Temple of Hadrian. With Artemis, goddess of fortune, above the front entrance and Medusa beyond with her arms open wide protecting the city from evil spirits.

16. Istanbul, (Grand Bazaar), Turkey Saturday 23rd June 2001

I am lost in Istanbul's wonderful and bizarre Grand Bazaar, an experience not to be missed. A sketcher's paradise in which one is constantly plied with water and Turkish tea. It is a real theatrical performance with constant cries of: 'This way please,' 'Best carpets here,' 'Lady lady,' and so on. I may drink the bazaar's Turkish tea reserves dry though, as I could stay here for decades. You can buy just about anything here, although antique pewter, copper and gold don't come cheap!

17. Istanbul, (Hagia Sophia and Blue Mosque), Turkey Thursday 28th June 2001

So a little over half way through my journey – and into my next sketchbook. At the top of my hotel I have found this fabulous view of the Blue Mosque and the Hagia Sophia staring at each other across the Istanbul rooftops. I find Istanbul completely intoxicating and full of wonderful people. When I draw I am often offered water or apple tea and there is a limitless list of things to sketch – fabulous Turkish baths, all the mosques, the mighty Bosphorus, the markets and, and, and…

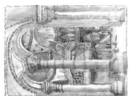 

18a. Istanbul, (Inside the Hagia Sophia), Turkey Thursday 28th June 2001
It is 1,500-years-old and totally breath-taking. The enormous dome seems to float high above, with glimmering gold mosaic all around. Home to Byzantine Christendom then Ottoman Islam.

18b. Istanbul, (The Spice Market), Turkey Saturday 30th June 2001
The Spice Market or Egyptian Bazaar is as colourful, chaotic and wonderful as the Grand Bazaar and the people as friendly and fascinating as ever. I love Turkey, hope I'm back soon.

19a. Kerman, (James Mosque), Iran Tuesday 3rd July 2001
Today I felt very privileged, because some of the tile-workers who are restoring the amazing Jame Mosque showed me their workshop so I could see how it is all done – very beautiful.

19b. Kerman, (Bazaar), Iran Tuesday 3rd July 2001
In the Vakil Tea house, a restored bathhouse or hammam, it is an oasis of calm from all the hubbub of the bazaar. I was invited to share tea with an Iranian couple which was very nice.

20. Arg-e Bam, Iran Thursday 5th July 2001

The modern day city of Bam now lies outside the walls of the ancient city of Arg-e Bam. The citadel is quite out of this world and completely compelling, even while drawing this in the soaring early morning heat, shrouded in my long black dress, melting. Now the only inhabitants of this amazing city are the restoration workers, the ladies in the gatehouse tea room – who make great cooked eggs – and the odd inquisitive lizard and bird.
Although badly damaged in the 2003 earthquake, it is being sympathetically restored.

21a. Shiraz, Iran Monday 9th July 2001
Shiraz Bazaar is wonderful and goes on for miles, incorporating mosques and teahouses and just about everything you could think of. In one of its many Aladdin's caves...

21b. Esfahan, Iran Wednesday 11th July 2001
The symphony of clanging metal suddenly got louder and louder. Turning the corner I found myself in the Copper Bazaar, where these amazing men, many quite elderly, are busily crafting their amazing pots and in this case vessels the size of a small boat – brilliant!

22a. Tashkent, Uzbekistan Sunday 15th July 2001
All change and on to Uzbekistan. Visiting this wonderful home in Tashkent filled with all the pots and tiles that I could ever dream of. The whole house is lovingly restored.

22b. Khiva, Uzbekistan Wednesday 18th July 2001
Inside the Juma Mosque in Khiva. It is a forest of 218 wooden columns on concrete bases, a few originals from the 10th Century, but most from the 18th Century onwards.

23. Khiva, Uzbekistan Thursday 19th July 2001

Khiva or more particularly Itchan Kala, inside the old city walls, is like a living museum. There are no ordinary shops or businesses giving that busy bustle and as it is outside tourist season it all seems a little sad to me. Still it is incredibly beautiful and its quietness makes it a restful place to be. This view shows the Islam-Khodja Minaret on the right, Pahlavan Mahmud Mausoleum, with its beautiful turquoise dome and then the Djuma Minaret on the left, with an array of other important things in between too!

24. Jodphur, (Surajpol, Meherengarh Fort), India Wednesday August 8th 2001

As a woman travelling alone I'm finding India a little overwhelming. So today, it is a relief to be up here at the Meherangarh Fort, where things are a little calmer and everyone is more intrigued by my drawing than by me. This sketch is the Suraj Pol entrance. All the courtyards and palaces of the Fort are interwoven and with the vibrant colours of the women's saris and the men's turbans, it is a sight of great beauty. Sudden fantastic bursts of colour as large groups of Indians of different castes appear and disappear through the layers of the fort...

25. Jodphur, (Meherengarh Fort), India Thursday 9th August 2001

Today I am high up on the ramparts of the Meherengarh Fort overlooking the old town, famously painted the various hues of bright blue Brahmin colours. I think I'm sitting close to the Loha Pol Gate, with its infamous row of Sati handprints. The most recent of these are the marks of the Maharaja Man Singh's widows, who threw themselves on to his funeral pyre in 1843 – gruesome! It seems to me that 150 years on, for most women here their lot has not improved much... It's the monsoon season and the roads really do turn into rivers.

26a. Temple at Ranakpur, India Friday 10th August 2001
Ranakpur – home to one of the largest, most ornate Jain temples in India. Supported by a forest of marble columns, this temple complex is incredibly ornate with every surface finely sculpted.

26b. Udaipur, (The Tailor), India Monday 13th August 2001
I'm getting a pair of trousers made, based on my old ones, which are almost falling apart now. The tailor performs small miracles on this wonderful old sewing machine.

27. Udaipur, (View across Lake Pichola), India Monday 13th – 17th August 2001

This is the view from the top of the haveli where I am staying in Udaipur. I've been drawing it in between rain showers and hot sunshine. This haveli has been my sanctuary and Udaipur is the city which has convinced me to stay in India and not run away back home. I still find it hard going, but have met some lovely people who have made it easier. I find it difficult to marry such a beautiful view with some of the hard things just around the corner.

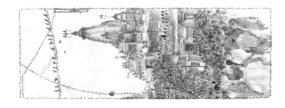

28. Udaipur, (Khrishna's Birthday), India Monday 13th August 2001

Today is Krishna's birthday. Last night at midnight the Jagdish temple was absolutely packed, but this evening's celebrations are even bigger. The whole square outside the temple is filled well beyond capacity as people watch teams of human pyramids compete to win a 5,000 rupee booty, which is hanging high above the square. It's amazing that no one has been seriously injured, as each pyramid collapses one after another. Finally the booty is lowered a little and one daring team grabs the pot. The lucky pigeons get the best view.

29. Jagmandir Island, Udaipur, India Wednesday August 15th 2001

An atmospheric monsoon day today. I took a boat ride on the serene Lake Pichola to Jagmandir Island, just in time as the heavens opened and the dark clouds leapt over the mountains unannounced and shrouded the landscape in a mysterious mist. Despite the chaotic weather, sketching here has provided me with a few hours of calm. In this picture you can just about see the City Palace and Jagniwas Island, home to the iconic Lake Palace Hotel.

30a. Udaipur, (View from the Paper Shop), India Friday August 17th 2001
Sketched from inside a paper shop where I've bought some handmade paper books. From my refuge I can capture the chaos out in the street – elephants, donkeys and sacred cows…

30b. Udaipur, (Women Washing), India Saturday 18th August 2001
India is still an assault on all the senses, all the time. But from the haven of my haveli you can look down on the ghats, women washing clothes, the boys washing themselves and swimming.

31. Kathmandu, (Durbar Square), Nepal Friday 24th – Saturday 25th August 2001

Although I'm quite worn out now, Nepal is worth the wait and all the effort. Although there is at least as much poverty here as there was in India, Nepal feels more gentle and calm. Durbar Square is seemingly strewn with shrines, temples, statues and the rest – it is a spectacular place. Pure inspiration for architects and town planners alike I think. Monkeys and mosquitoes are making mischief. A monkey climbed on to one of the roofs and threw down tiles, which smashed on the ground, whilst the mosquitoes simply concentrated on me.

32a. Kathmandu, (From the Royal Palace), Nepal Friday 24th August 2001
The view from the eighth of the nine-storied Basantapur tower of the Royal Palace looking across Nasal Chowk to Panchmukhi Hanuman Temple and the massive Taleju temple beyond.

32b. Kathmandu, (Swayambunath Temple), Nepal Sunday 26th August 2001
Up 365 gravity-defying stone steps to Swayambunath or more appropriately the Monkey Temple. The monkeys are incredible and fearless – and will grab most things grabbable!

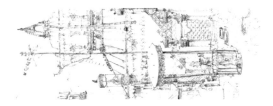

33. Kathmandu, (Unfinished), Nepal Monday 27th August 2001

A note 14 years on: For some reason I had to leave sketching this early and I didn't make any notes at the time. It was somewhere in Central Kathmandu or just across the river in Patan, the second city. I've included it, as it shows all the intricate details emerging from the temple and this graceful, mysterious, almost renaissance like statue with ornate canopy 'sauntering' over to the other stupas and shrines. Let me know if you recognise the location...

34. Bhaktapur, Nepal Wednesday 29th August 2001

I've reached Bhaktapur, otherwise known as Bhadgoan, from village of rice to city of devotees. Nepal's third city is a time capsule from medieval times and set nestled in the foothills of the Himalayas. This is Tachupal Tole, probably the oldest part of town, looking across to the Dattatraya Temple. Life is in full swing in the square below, the bright-eyed crippled beggar, whom I am told lives with his parents up the road, doing the rounds, people selling things, couples of men everywhere, kids playing and so on.

My adventure began with a train ride from London to Paris and only subtle cultural differences with which to contend. In Italy I received wonderfully warm hospitality from friends, friends of friends, and friends of friends of friends – truly 'bella Italia'. Greece was all a bit greek to me and more than once I went on long detours through misunderstanding. Turkey was wonderfully diverse and vibrant. With tea on tap, what more could I ask for? In Iran I quickly got used to my 'not-so-little' black dress and found the hospitality shown to me quite humbling.

Uzbekistan was a country in transition, heat exhaustion and food poisoning did not help, but the vodka did! India was an assault on all the senses, all the time. Culture shock well and truly hit me here. It is a country of extremes where heaven and hell exist like oil and water – karma chaos. In Nepal medieval and modern life combined in a wonderful vibrancy – stone Buddhas and incarnations, stupas and other edifices nestled in amongst washing lines and 'internet access here' signs. Humanity in its heritage and a journey of a lifetime.